#NaPoWriMo Fail

2022

EUGENETTE MORIN

Because though we may try,
we sometimes fail ....

Published, illustrated, and edited by:
Coach Gen Editions
Montreal, Canada

Dedication

To all who dare to try
And shout their failures to the sky
Take heart, you are not alone
It's all right, we grow on

Table of Contents

Author's Note

I was taking 4 university courses that semester but learned about an April challenge, and so, I resolved to take on #NaPoWriMo 2022. Just in case it's new to you as well, April is National Poetry Month. The cat in the poem 'Another One of Those' is mine, her name is Okra.

The Challenge

Write a poem a day for 30 days

I figured, one a day – that's not too bad!
I can do this, I've got this
I can handle it
It's only one and it doesn't have to be long; look at haikus.
Well, I shot myself in the foot …
Because I managed to write 29 … and not 30!

They were originally published on my blog:
https://thecoatofmanypockets.com/?page_id=52

I chose to publish this unsuccessful attempt for two reasons:
1. Failure is a new opportunity
2. I will try again … the next one will be called…

#NaPoWriMo Success

But for now, welcome to ….

#NaPoWriMo Fail 2022

Here we Go – Here we Are!

First DAY

Here we go
The first day of the beginning
is always the next day of the rest.

Spiraling up to the sky,
or is it ...
winding down from the clouds?

Because the last day of the ending
Is never the next day of what's left
And yet, here we are!

Spires Powered Sports

Spires Powered Sports or Spired Powers Sported .... who knows?

For NaPoWriMo's daily dose

Inspired inspiration transpires empires

Empowered empoweration inpowers transpowers

Transported transportation insports emsports

I Didn't Feel Like It

I just didn't feel like typing

I didn't feel like it

So, it's a one-day-late-post

I wrote in my notebook

I followed the challenge

Of one poem a day,

Every, every, every single day

I didn't skip a day...

But I didn't feel like typing

Choices in the Making

Waiting to be made – choices, in the making

In the waking hours of the waning night

Choices can fade in brightness

In the crowning kilometer of the lightening ride

Choices can be brought to lightness

Choices in the making of the crossroads

of the crosshairs in the crossings of the

intersecting intersections of my choice-a-lities!

In the opening doors of the closing meetings

Voices can alter vibrations

In the primal cry of the mother's soothing

Voices and choices can blend in dimensions

Cube Cubed Cubes

A study in 3's = 27
3 words of 3 syllables that are 3 words themselves

To get her,

Ans, we red

At ten dance

Stories – Day or Night

If there should be a story's day

A tale's tally and a fable's foibles

An adventure's exploits with soaring vocals

If there should be a story's night

A dream's image and reverie reverbs

A chimera's illusion with wordless blurbs

If there should be a story to be heard

to be said, to be listened to, to be told

Cubes Squared

Conversations lost,

Unheard amidst the

Bustling noises,

Engulfing voices

Since it seems like ... forever

Since it seems like ... forever

Quizzical confusion

Ultimately discovers within

All the cacophony,

Rare moments of clarity

Enlightening spaces

Deeply hidden from view

Another one of those

Again, another one, why?

Give me something new

Give me something juicy

Stop with all that is meowy

Stop with all the cat news

———

Again, not another one of those?

Oh no! Will this nightmare never end?

Give me something dreamy

Give me something lucid

Stop with all this kitteny cupid

Stop with all the cat stories

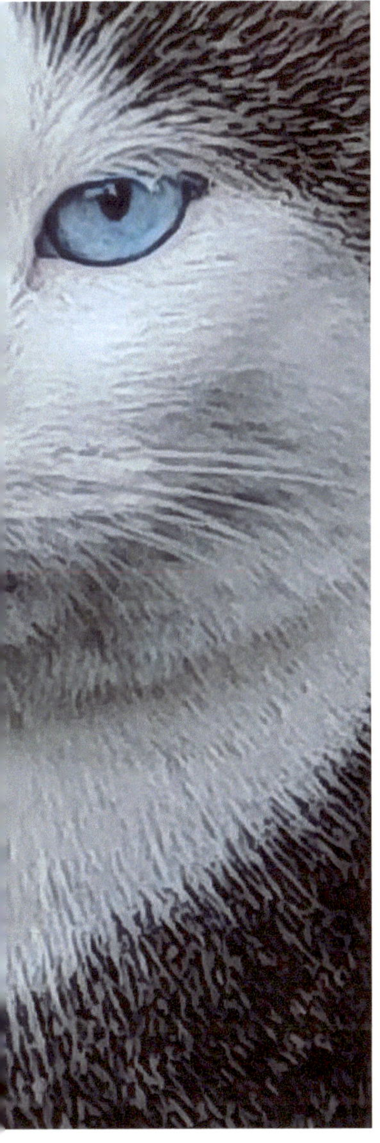

Really, another one of those?

Again, and more, and what for

Give me something other

Give me something barky

Stop with all the cat stories

Stop with those disasters

——

No, no more, I will listen to not

Another of those stories

Give me, at least once

Stories of a dog or maybe a tree

Stories of a mouse on a journey

Anything to avoid

Another one of those stories

Come Celle-Là
Comme une of those

Dew a journée rose come une of those

Il faisait beautiful, si hot, si hot (fan)

I was sweeting ... oops, I mean swayting

En tout cas, you know what I mean (smile)

C'était une blue day come celle-là

It was pas cool, and so froid, so froid

Je tremblois ... oops, J'veux dire tromblais

In any case, tu sais ce que j'veux dire

Il fallait une umbrelle,

We needed a parka

Pendant une blue journée rose

come une of those

with two languages in tandem together

1980's Hair Routine

Shampoo, repeat, condition, under scalding heat

Slather and massage mousse or gel into scalp

Dry with blistering hot air

With a very large diffuser

    Next, spray a ton of hairspray over it

    Curl or straighten with your scorching iron

    Add hairspray – lots of it

Tease the hell out of every strand you can find

Keep curling – straightening as needed

Lift with a long-pick-tooth comb, spray

Lift-spray here, lift-spray there, and again

Pat, pat, pat it all down but not too much

And get to work, work, work it

It Drives Me Mad

It drives me mad
It drives me batty
How he hates baths
And she hates nappies

It drives me bonkers
It drives me zonkers
How loud are his cries
And strident are hers

It drives me nuts
It drives me wild
How he bellows displeasure
And she follows louder

No need for clean
Just let them sleep
No need to be clean
Just time for sleep

The Day I was Born

The day I was born
Half a century plus a year
A half-century I've been here
And even a year more and above
I've been still here, and there, and here, love

***

Today, early morning, very early
It was the day when I chose
I came and said hello there, dearie
It was early morning when she rose

****

All that time ago
A half-century plus one to grow
That's how long I've been here
And how long I've been there, and back here

****

I came early and yet so late
Wait, hours, days, and weeks, she'd wait
I could've been here with Spring
But I came in the early morning!

Strain Train – Train Brain

There are all these strains
Which is best for my brains?

How about the sativa?
It's all a haze
It's a color, a fruit, a what?
Don't matter, it's a craze

How about the indica?
It's all a kush
It's a color, a fruit, a what?
Don't matter, it's not for your tush

We've got whites
Like widows and rhinos
We've got blues
Like berries and dreams
We've got reds, purples, and blacks
Like lights and beauties

All of the strain
on my brain
needs to train
for all these strain trains.

Phoneme and Morpheme

Tension – Ten Shun
Enjoying the tension
between syllable and word
morpheme and phoneme

Trad it ion al
TolE-Rants
Can ad a
de light ful
mode r-nit-y

Phoneme and morpheme
between sound and intent
enjoying the ten shun

Ap peal, a pear
A peel, ap pear
A peel appeals
A pear appears
Make what you will of it all

#NaPoWriMo Halfway Point

I admit it hasn't been easy

To have every day a new story

But I'm doing it

Every day there's a hit

This play, think and write starts with coffee

***

I disclose it's been quite a task

To come up with new things to ask

It creeps up on me

As it must daily

But I do not turn to the flask

Share WHERE?

————————————

There's stuff I've shared here

or there, that I've shared everywhere.

But then, there's the stuff that's only here

or there, that's only nowhere.

Share WHERE?

There's the junk I've served here

or there, that I've served anywhere.

And of course, there's the junk that's just here

or there, that's just wherever.

And ever and never and every … where

Because that's what it costs to share

every and any and no … where

Share WHERE?

How Shall We Live?

How shall we live?
In our dreams, in our visions...
A question from the sages
Of courage and decisions.
How shall we live?

> In our days, in our nights...
> How shall we summon them to life?

How shall we live?
With everyday intention.
A proposal from the mages
Of thoughts and intuition.
How shall we live?

> In our homes, in our lands
> How shall we keep it all alive?

Cattitude

Proudly coming out of the salon, her tri-color coat sleek,
brilliant,
dazzled every eye.
She strutted down the alley,
her tail high,
swaying along invitingly.
Her purr called every ear,
loud yet soft,
it resonated with pure satisfaction.
Almost as soft as the cloudy fur
she paraded and pranced
on her way home,
as soft as the enchantment
of her Spring transformation.
Under her spell, Viktor, Bad Boy, and Spike
followed behind sniffing
the heady perfume that emanated behind her.
As she got to her gate,
she turned,
and swishing her tail,
grinned at them.
She had it all
Cattitude – Strutting out of the Salon

Shape-Shifting Clouds in the Sky

Shape-shifting clouds in the sky

Taking a break for a while

Watching shapes drift along

Shape-shifting clouds in the sky

****

Wander forward lazily

There is a stretching kitty cat

Meander above leisurely

Hovering just like a bat

****

Watch the shape-shifting clouds in the sky

Lie down, relax, and read the blue

Like a book, your mind's the clue

To see shape-shifting clouds in the sky

Tristesse Profonde Enracinée

La sphère ne tourne plus rond
Les formes ne se reconnaissent plus
Les angles se sont
concrétisés
Le faux se voit adulé
Le vrai anéanti,
caché
Sous la domination
De plusieurs addictions
La communication
fragmentée
La discussion dirigée et digérée
La douleur de l'esprit
Le cœur trop meurtri
Déni de la conscience
Pour toutes les apparences
La peur, la guerre adulées
La sphère se meurt, oubliée
Tristesse profonde enracinée
Dans l'ombre de l'illusion
Qui invite la collision
Reconnaitre notre divinité
Ainsi que celle de la sphère
Ainsi que celle appelée Mère
Ainsi que celle nommée Nature
Et pour toutes nos progénitures

Every Once in ...

Every once in a Very LONG while

Long walked along the long road

Widely wandering with wanderlust

Wildly wondering in the wild-wild whirl

**

Because

**

Every once in a very LONG while

Long shuffled along the short shore

Sweetly sweeping by swallows

Swiftly swimming by swans

... a Very LONG while

It was just that

Every once in a Very LONG while

Long longed for the long lane

Lengthily lingering tracks of trains

Lastingly long-winded brack of brains

***

Every once in a VERY LONG while

Long longs for the open

Every once in a VERY LONG while

Falling Behind

Oh no, I'm falling behind
Can't type all time
Want a break from my pencil
***

Oh no, I wasn't the kind
To put off the rhyme
And go for the stencil
***

Oh no, I must have been blind
Thought I could sublime
Follow the protocol
***

Well now I'm in a bind
It's hardly benign
And simply not practical
***

Oh no, I'm falling behind
But you can still follow me

In the Lightness of Space

Wholly whole holy holes
Black and swirly
Shimmer and shimmy
In the lightness of space
***

Wholly whole holy holes
Clear and shiny
Flashing and flashy
In the weightlessness of space

In the weightlessness of space
Gaping and open
Curiously unhidden
Wholly whole holy holes
***

In the lightness of space
Weird and Strange
Circles and lozenges
Wholly whole holes

Maybe there are many
Wholly whole holy holes
Floating in the weightlessness of space
Black in the lightness of space

Dictionary – An Acrostic Poem

Definitions

In writing

Cover every page.

Thumbing through it,

I'm flabbergasted,

obviously amazed.

Nowhere can be found

Additional words

Real or Imagined

You know where to go

ABCDErian - Bubble's Travel Log: 26 Seconds of Life

A
Bubble blown by
Charlie carelessly,
Dew-like droplet,
Ever entertaining.
Floating fragility
Grazes grasses
Hones, hovers
Images immerge.
Jaunty jumps
Kite-like
Leaps,
Moving mostly
Nervously.
Other ones
Perhaps, pirouette
Saunter, slide
Topsy-turvy,
Unlike unique
Windsurfing
Xavier.
Your yonder,
Zany — ZAP!

Challenges Faced Hand in Hand

Challenges faced hand in hand
Always find an all-people's land
Sisters, brothers, friends, and foes
We all need to stop with the blows

***

Blows rain down from on high
The clouds are dark in the sky
Challenges faced with each other
Bring us closer together

***

Together we are always there
For life, for here and everywhere
We must join, unite, create
A world for all of us, no hate

***

Challenges faced hand in hand

Startling Sybil's Sibilance

Startling Sybil's stuttering stopped
Sporadically since springtime
Sounds, sparrows, squeals
Sybil's sighed softly
***

Surrounding streams sources
Sixteen, seventeen swans
Swimming splendidly serene
Sybil sees satisfaction

Swallows swoop skies
Soaring, surging starlings
Such soulful sights
Sybil sways side-to-side
***

Sybil's sputtering stopped
Since summertime songs
Slowly, silently, sunnily
Sybil smiles satisfaction

It's ALWAYS been YOU

My first breath
My first sight
All were you, you, you

My second touch
My second taste
All about you, you, you

My third sound
My third smell
Each a piece of you, you, you

My fourth wind
My fourth view
Each a part of you, you, you

My fifth caress
My fifth gusto
All about you, you, you

My sixth noise
My sixth aroma
All were you, you, you

My every murmur
My every vision
All were you, you, you

My every contact
My every flavor
All about you, you, you

My every melody
My every whiff
Has always been you, you, you
Will forever be you, you, you

LIFE, my one, true, constant love

LIFE, where would I be without you?

Every day – Heads in the Clouds

Every day – heads in the clouds

Walking through infinity

Sifting through immobility

of the mass of humanity

***

Every day – feet on the ground

Touching unknowable infinity

Wading upon security

of the constant ecology

***

Every day – body in the between

Probing eternal infinity

Sensing with vibration

of the open perception